I0409712

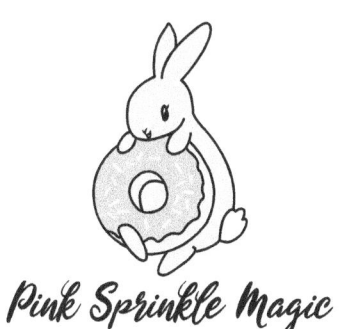

Pink Sprinkle Magic

Cute Kawaii Halloween

♡ Coloring Book ♡

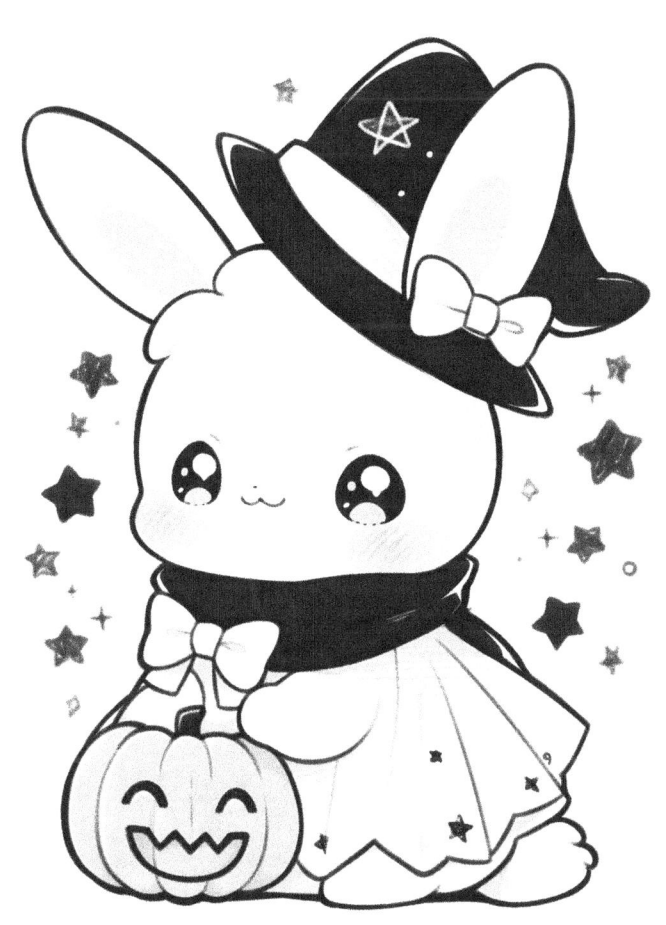

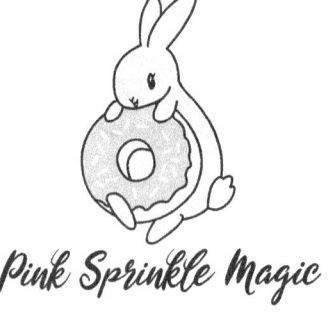

Pink Sprinkle Magic

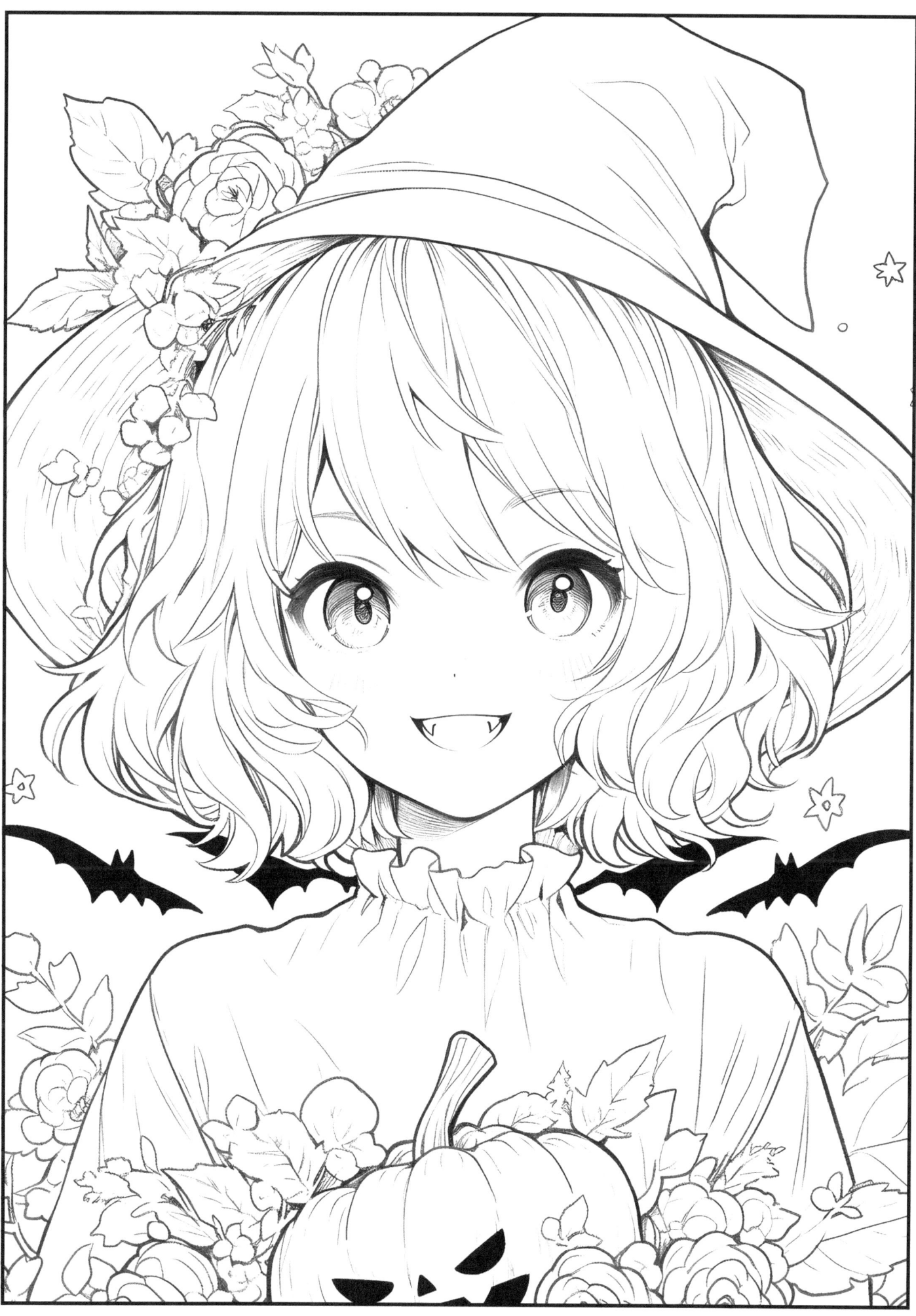

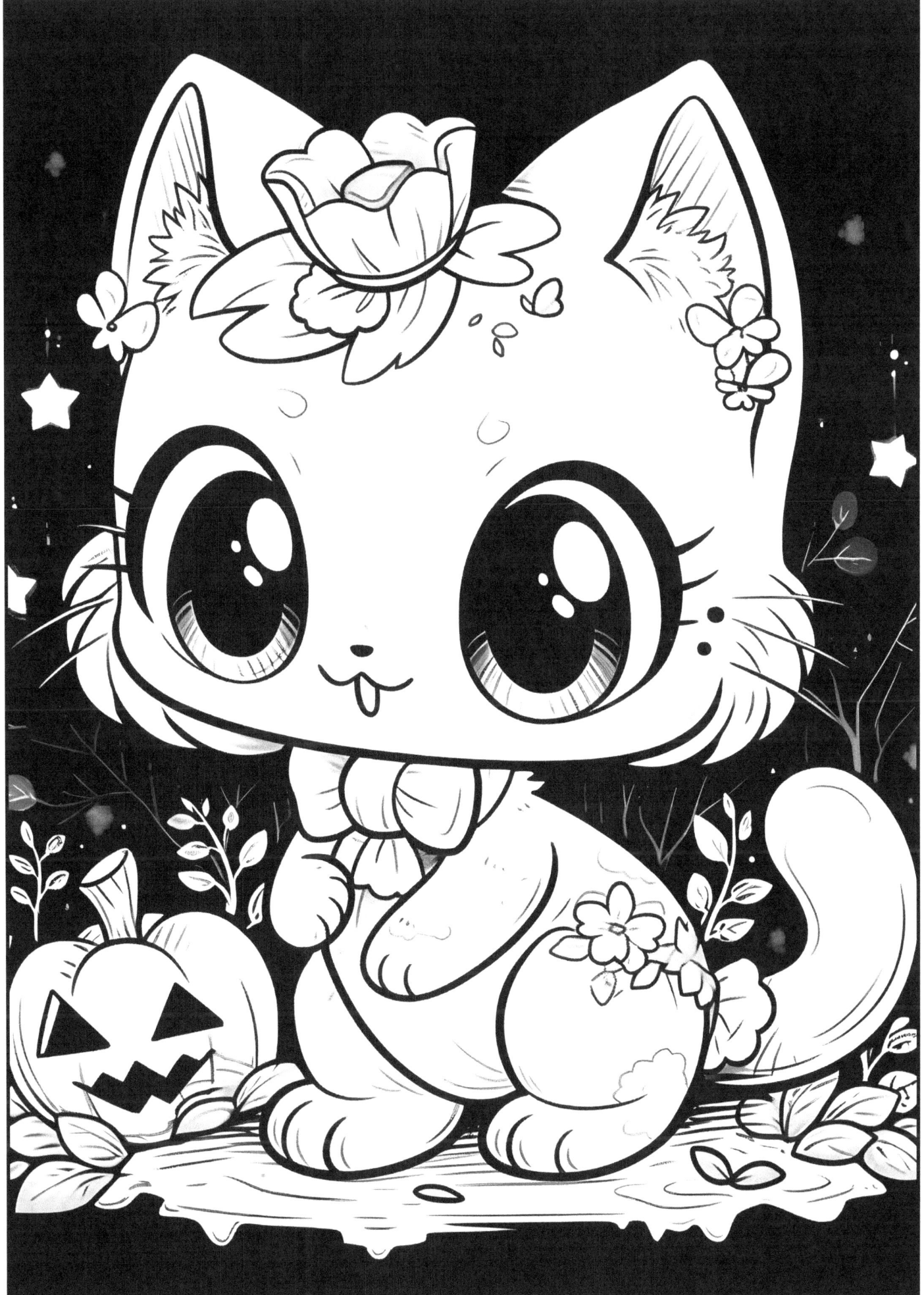

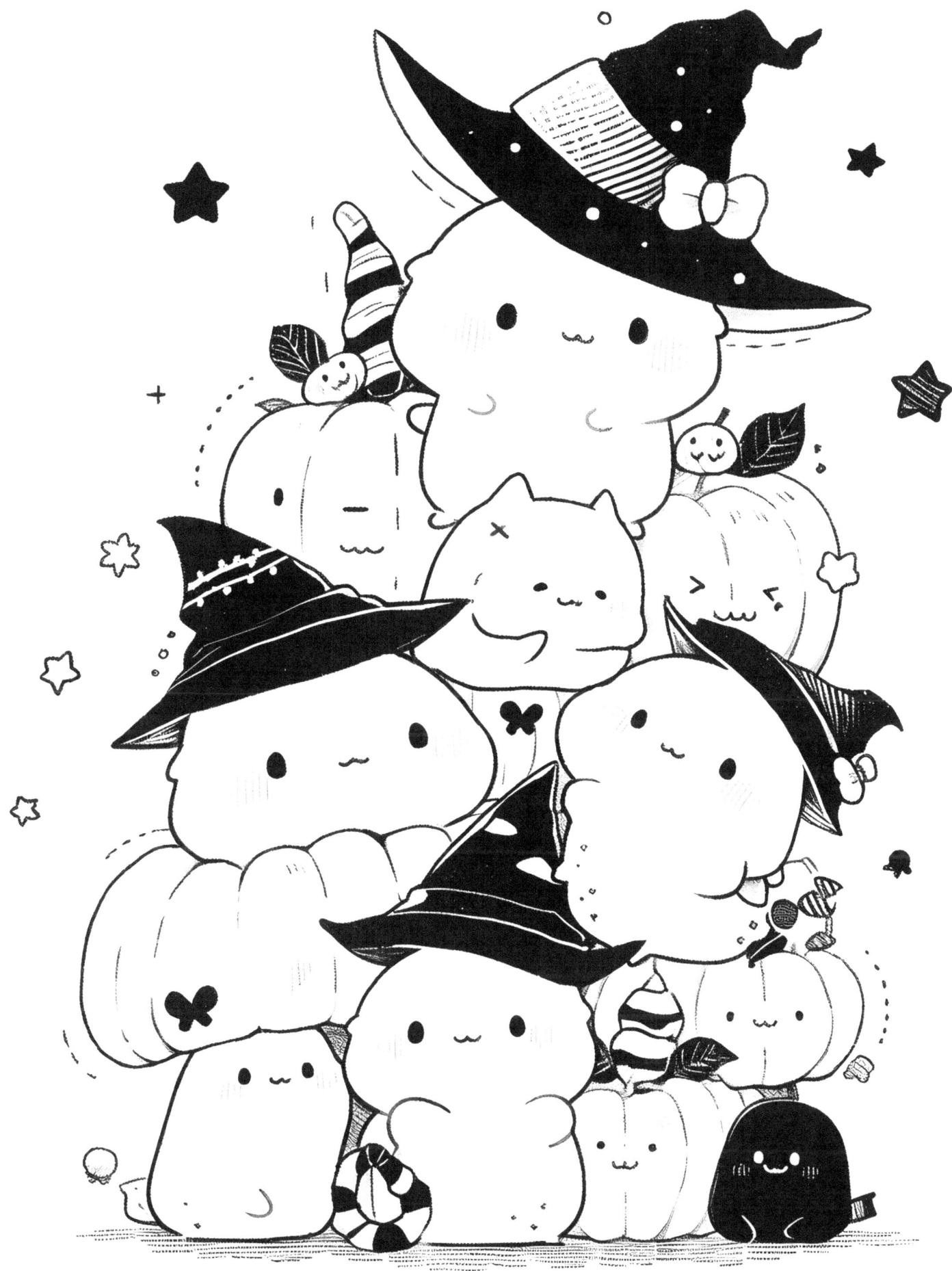

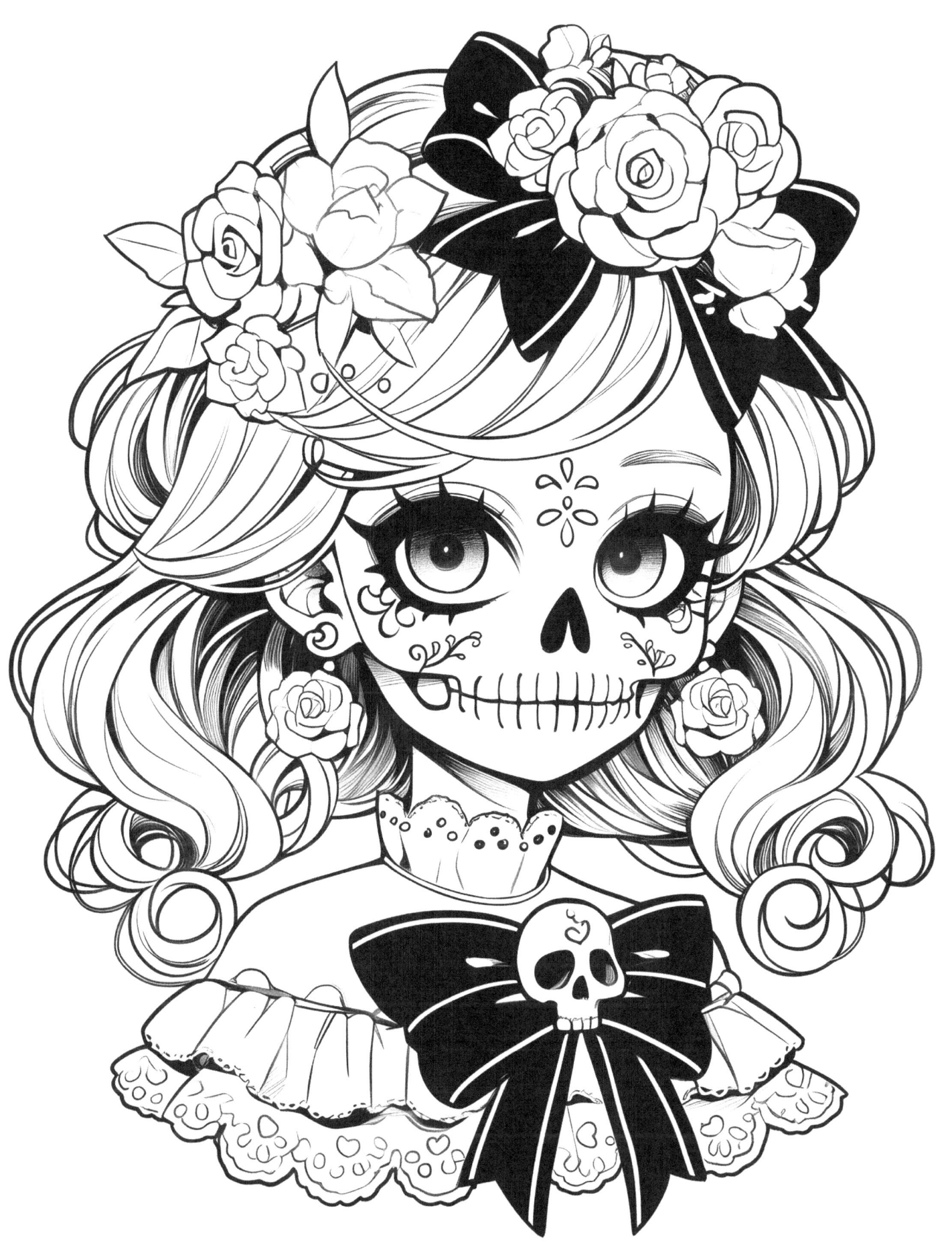

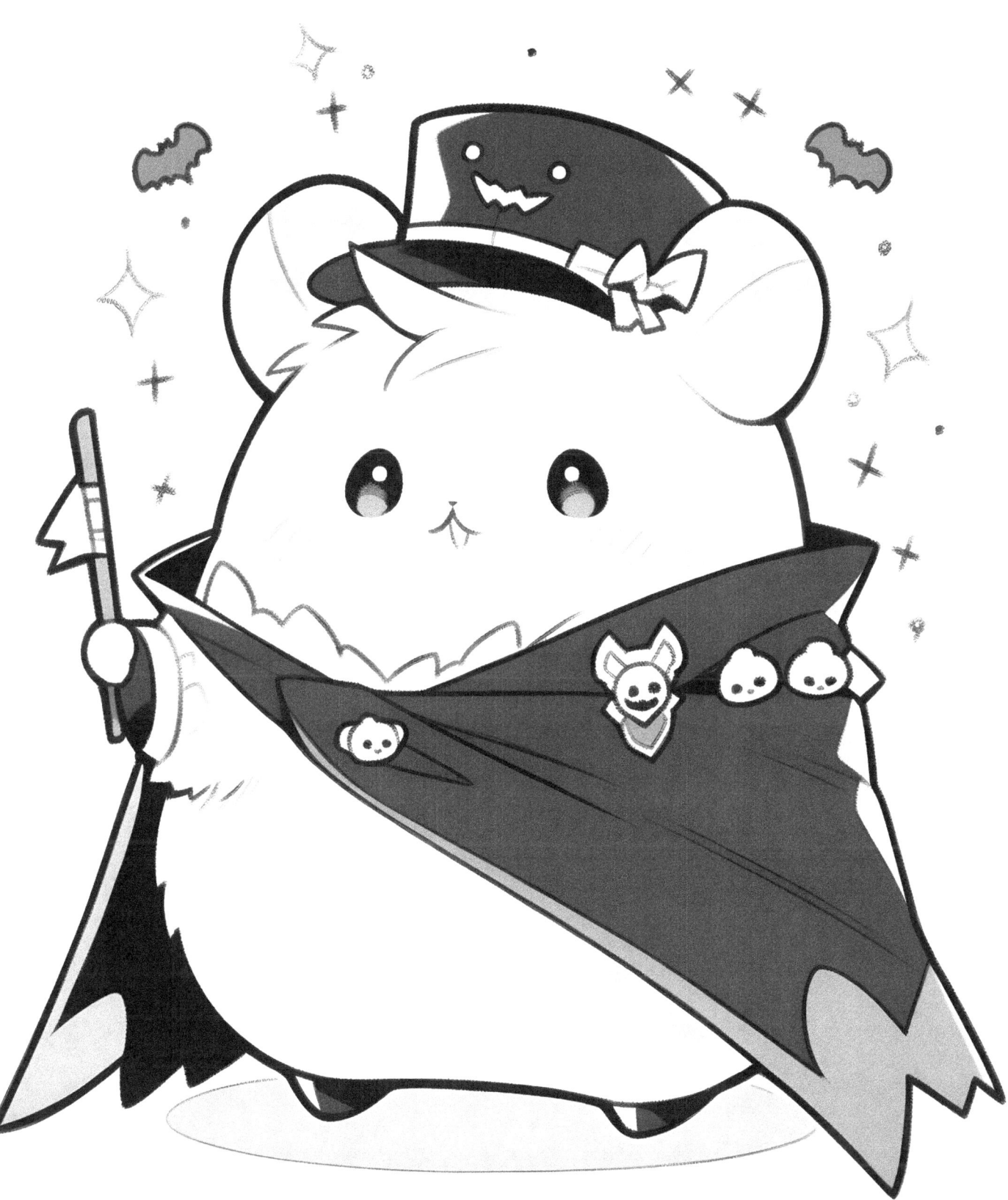

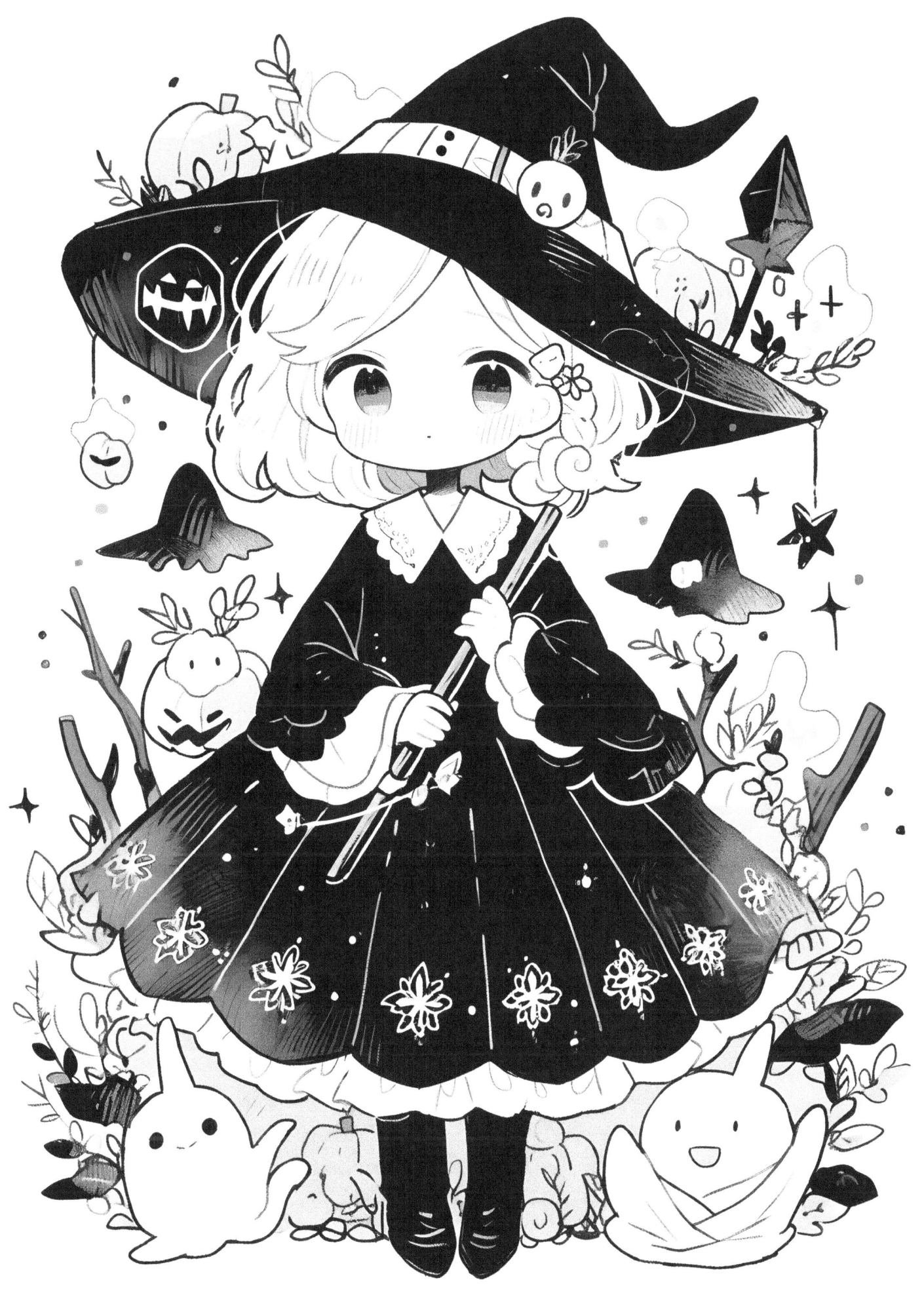

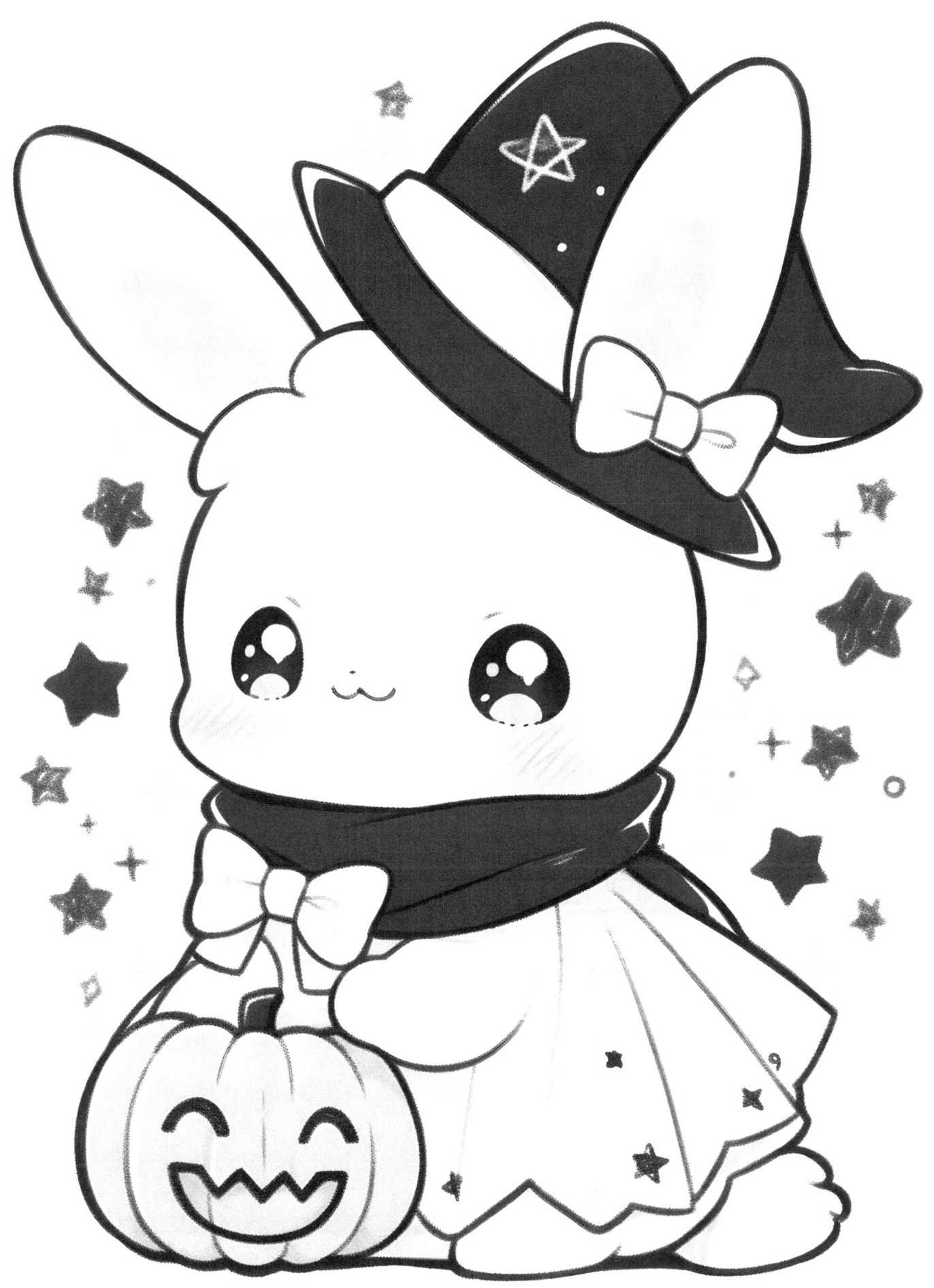

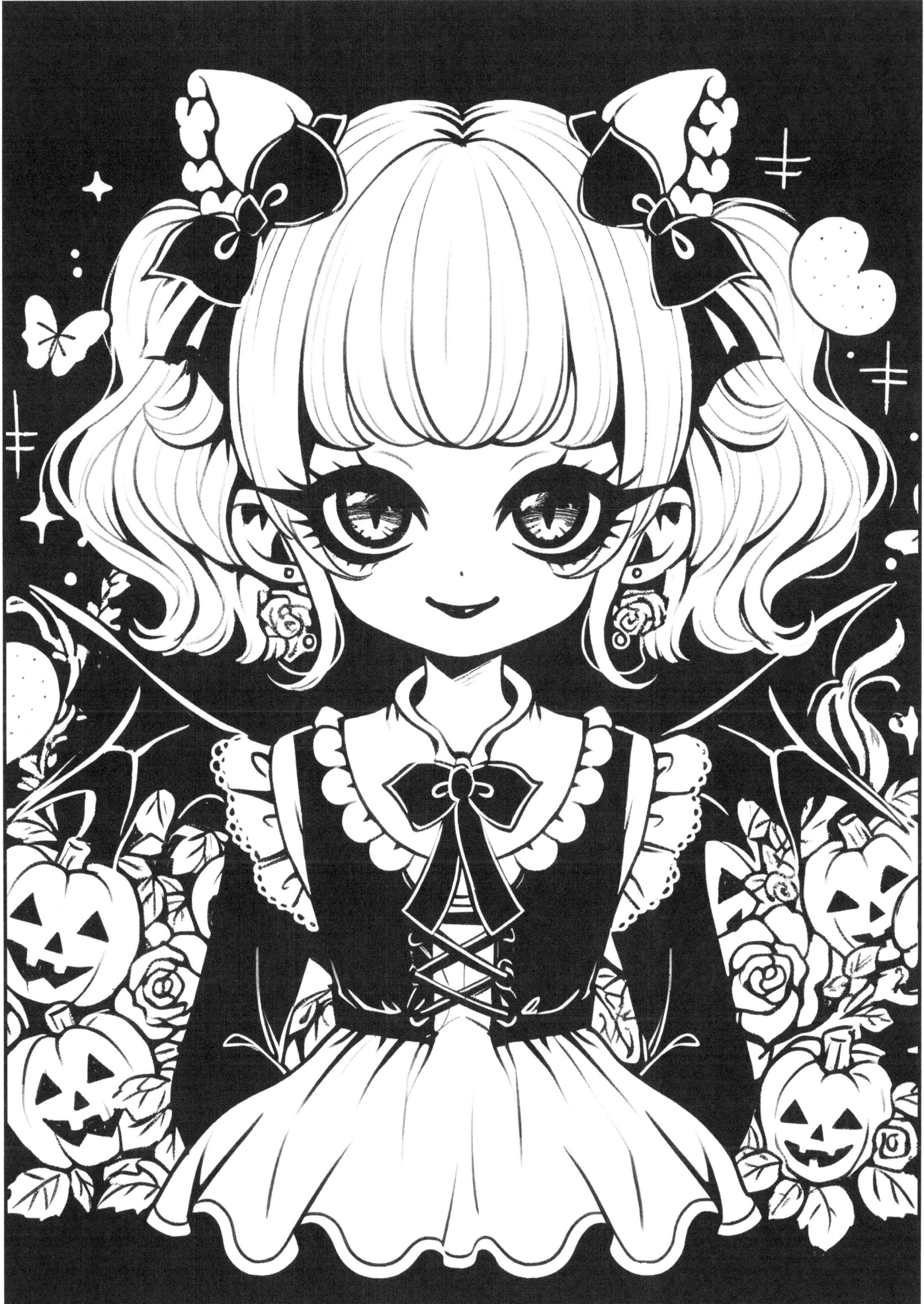

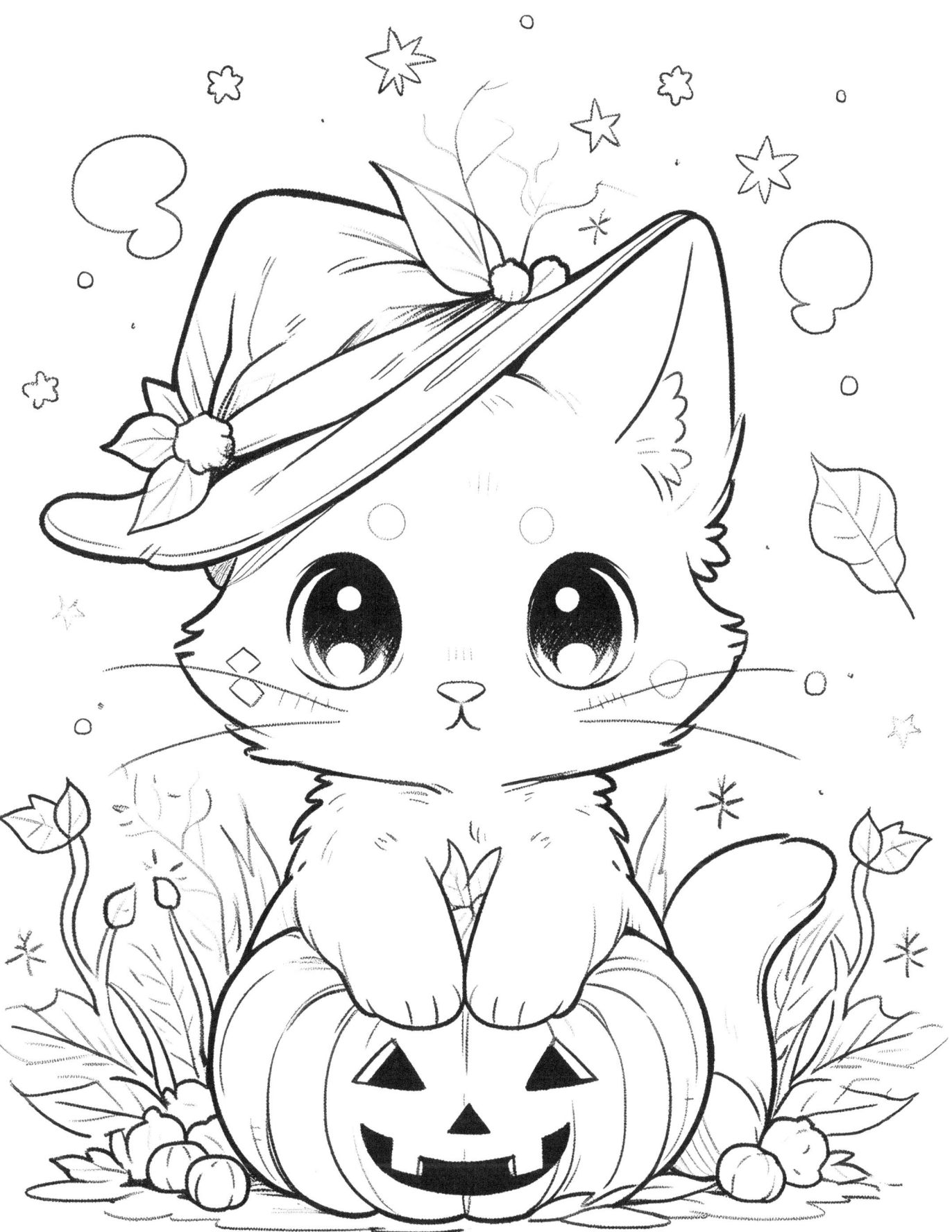

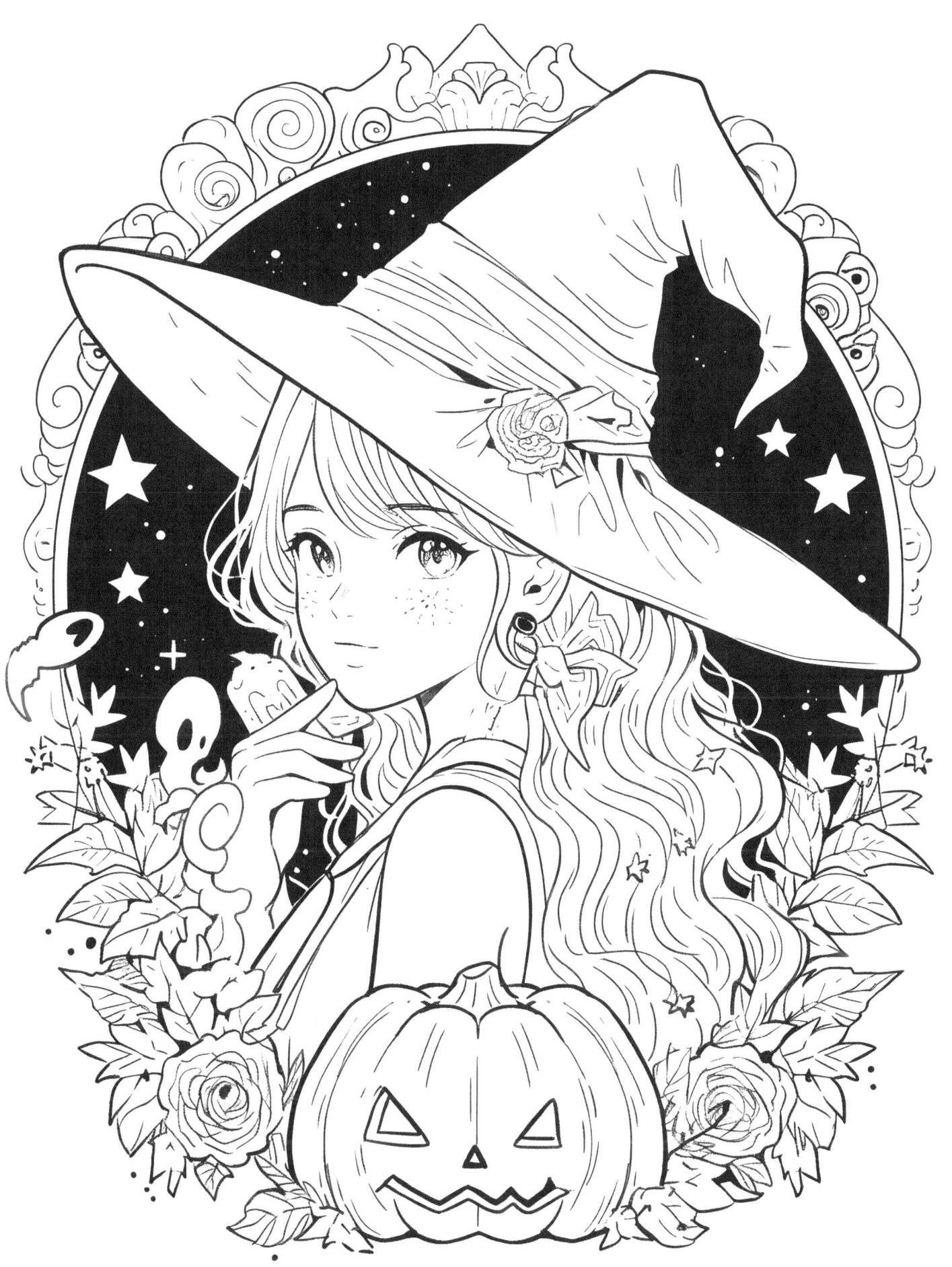

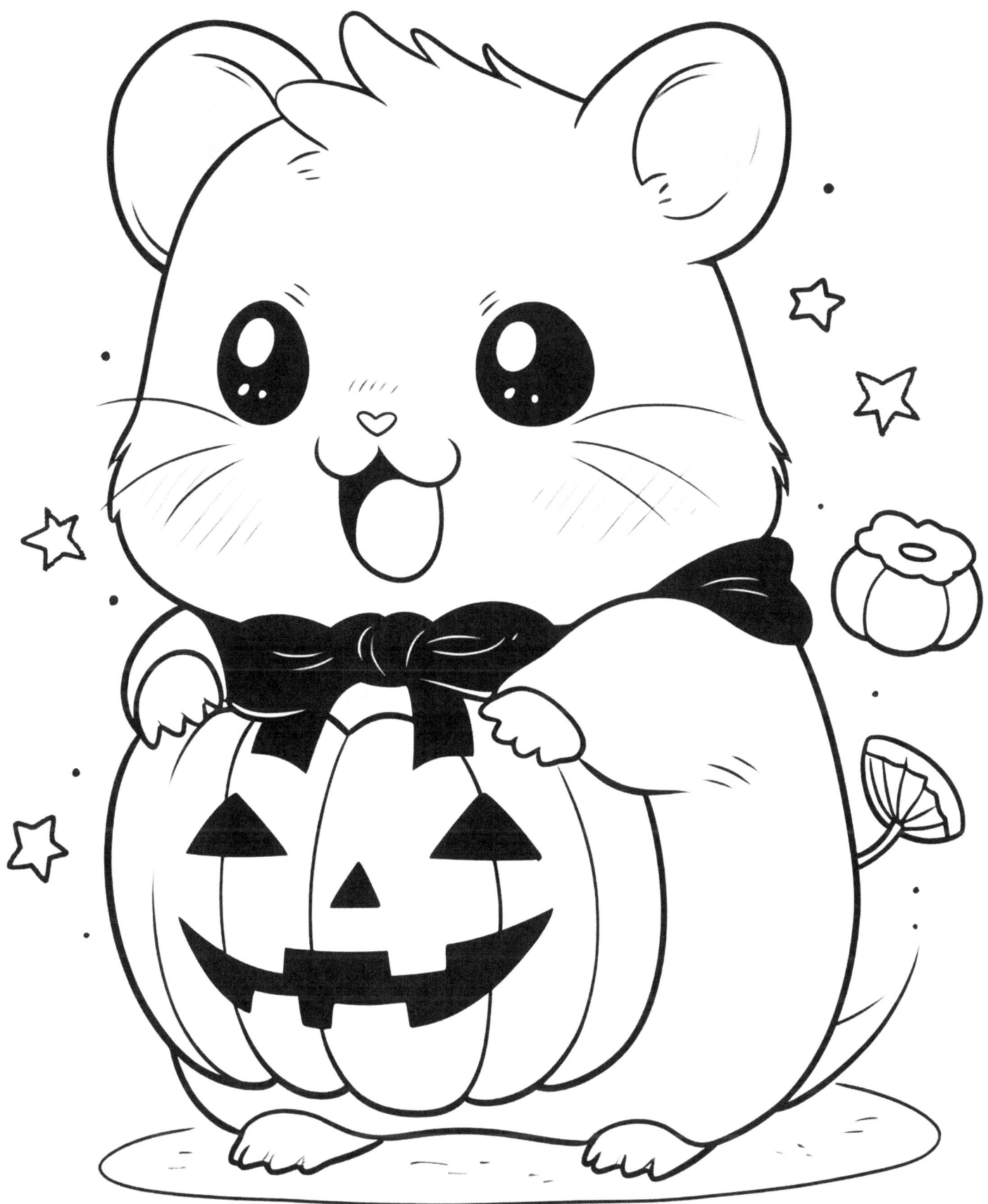

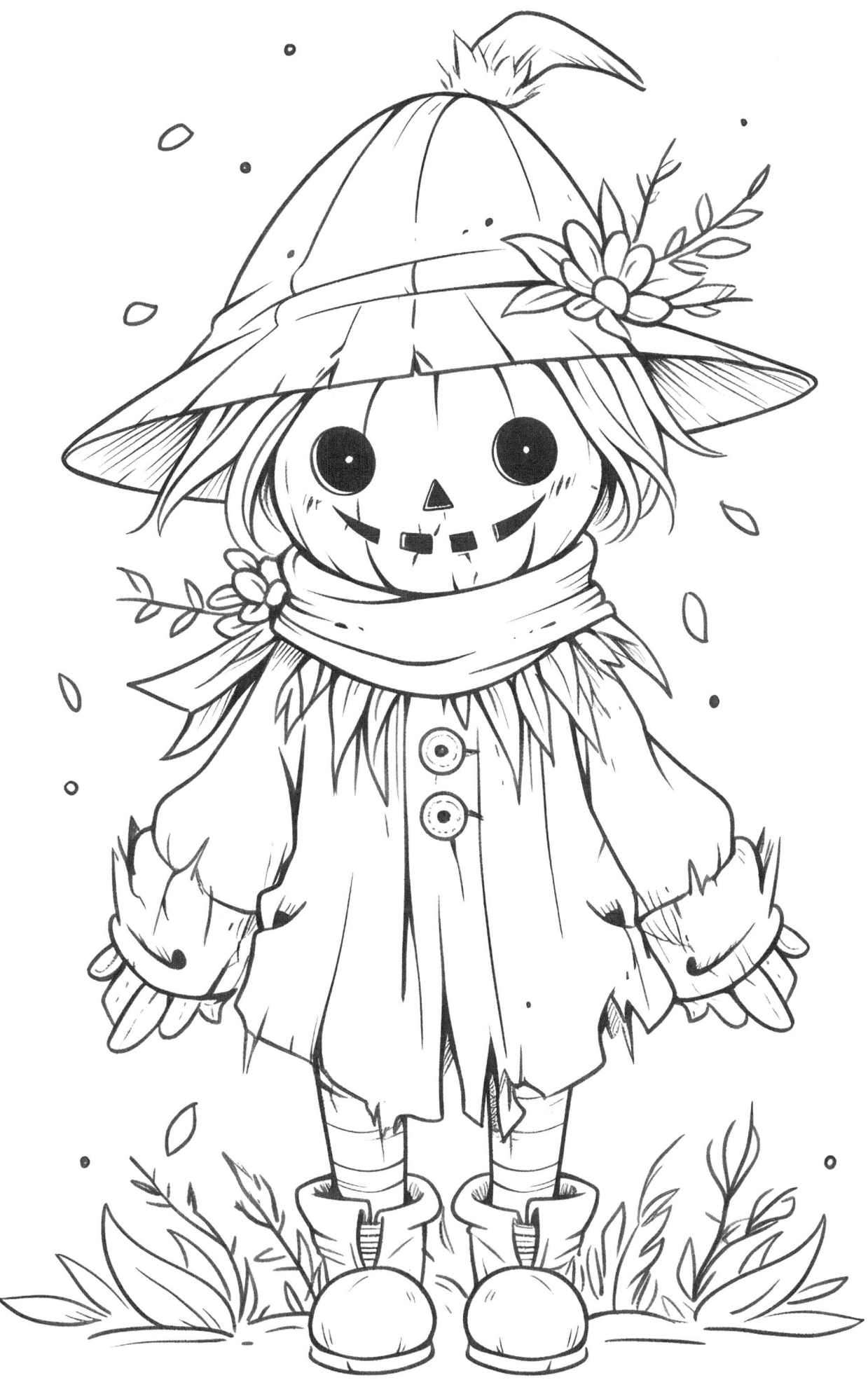

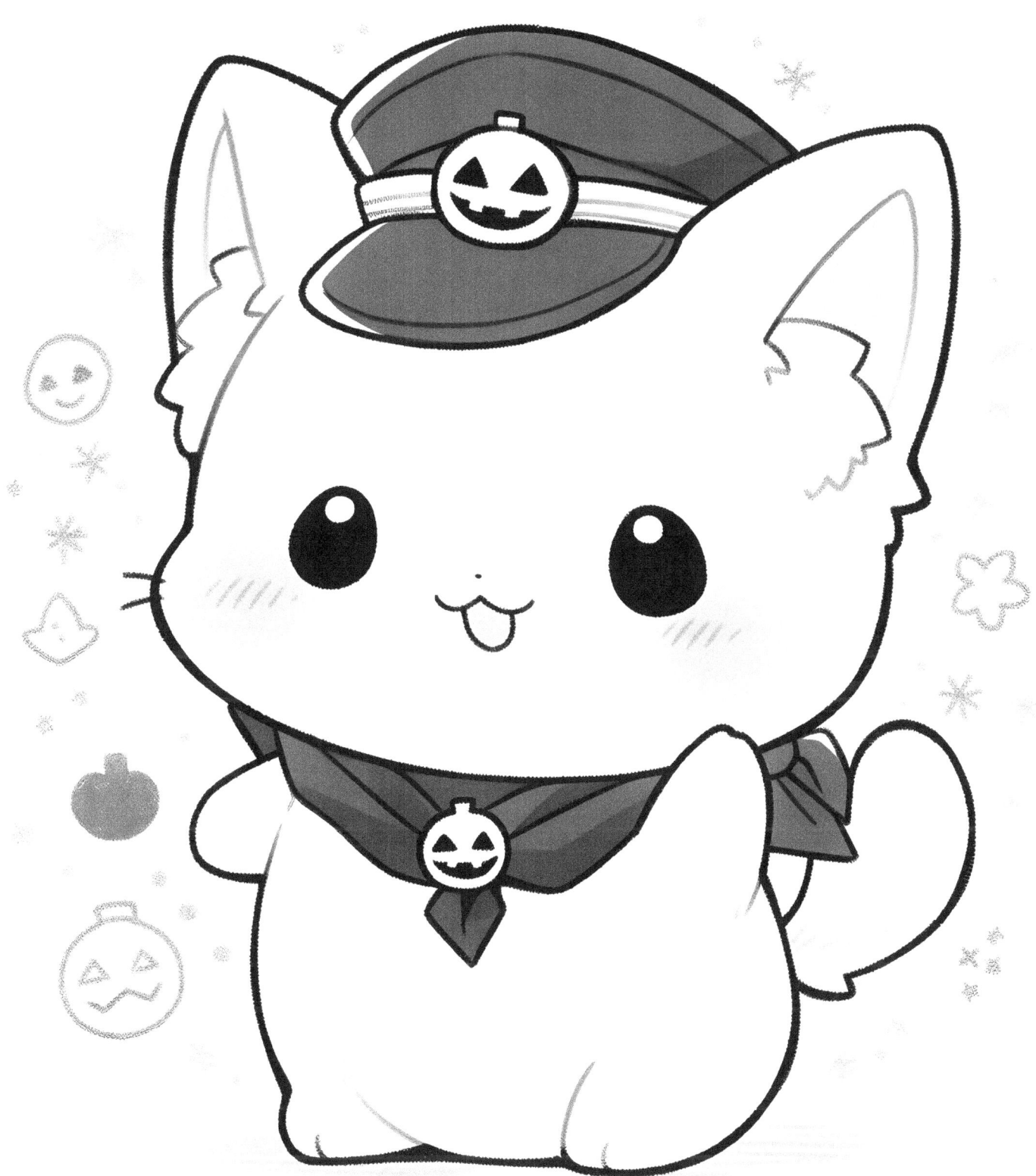

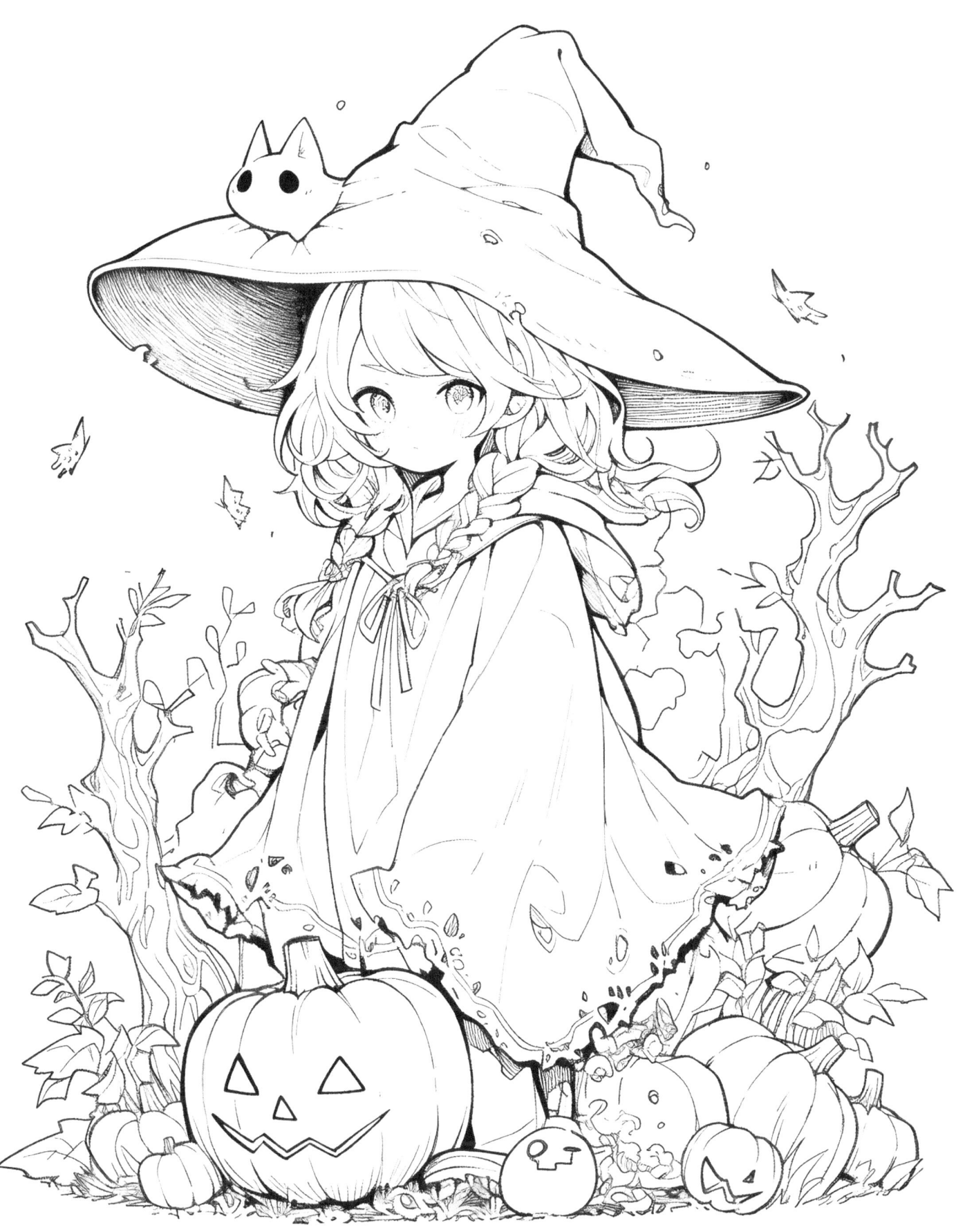

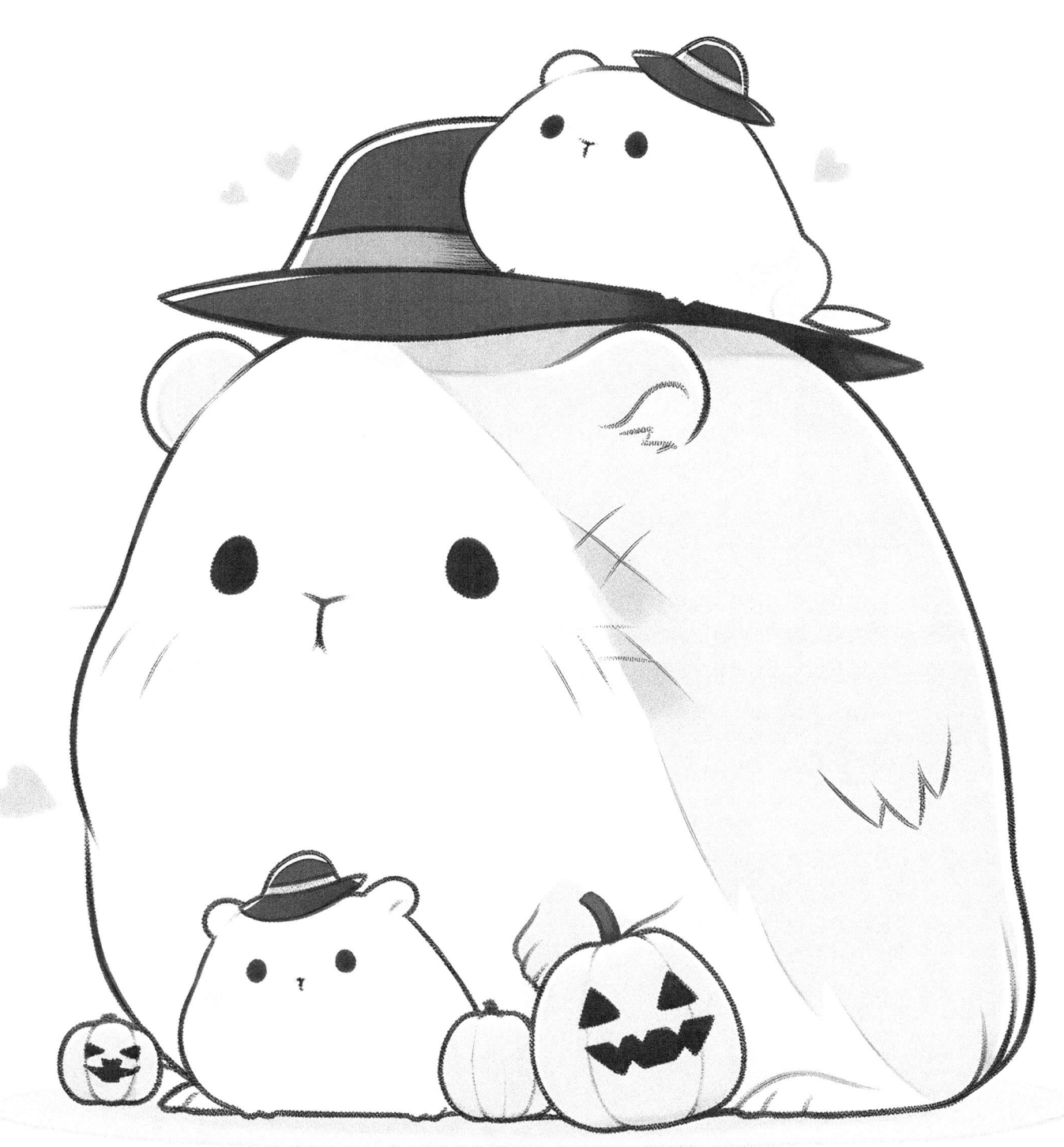

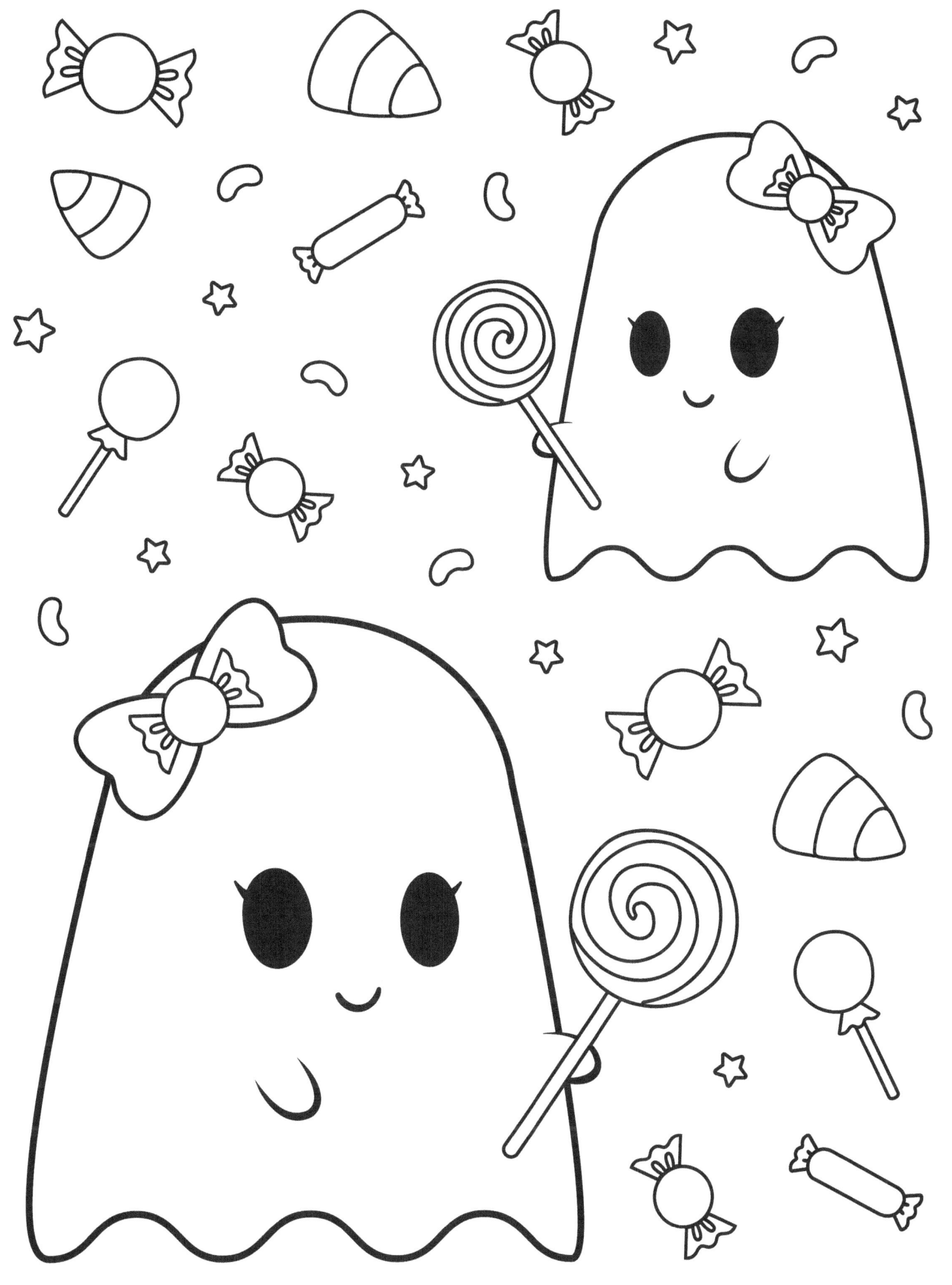

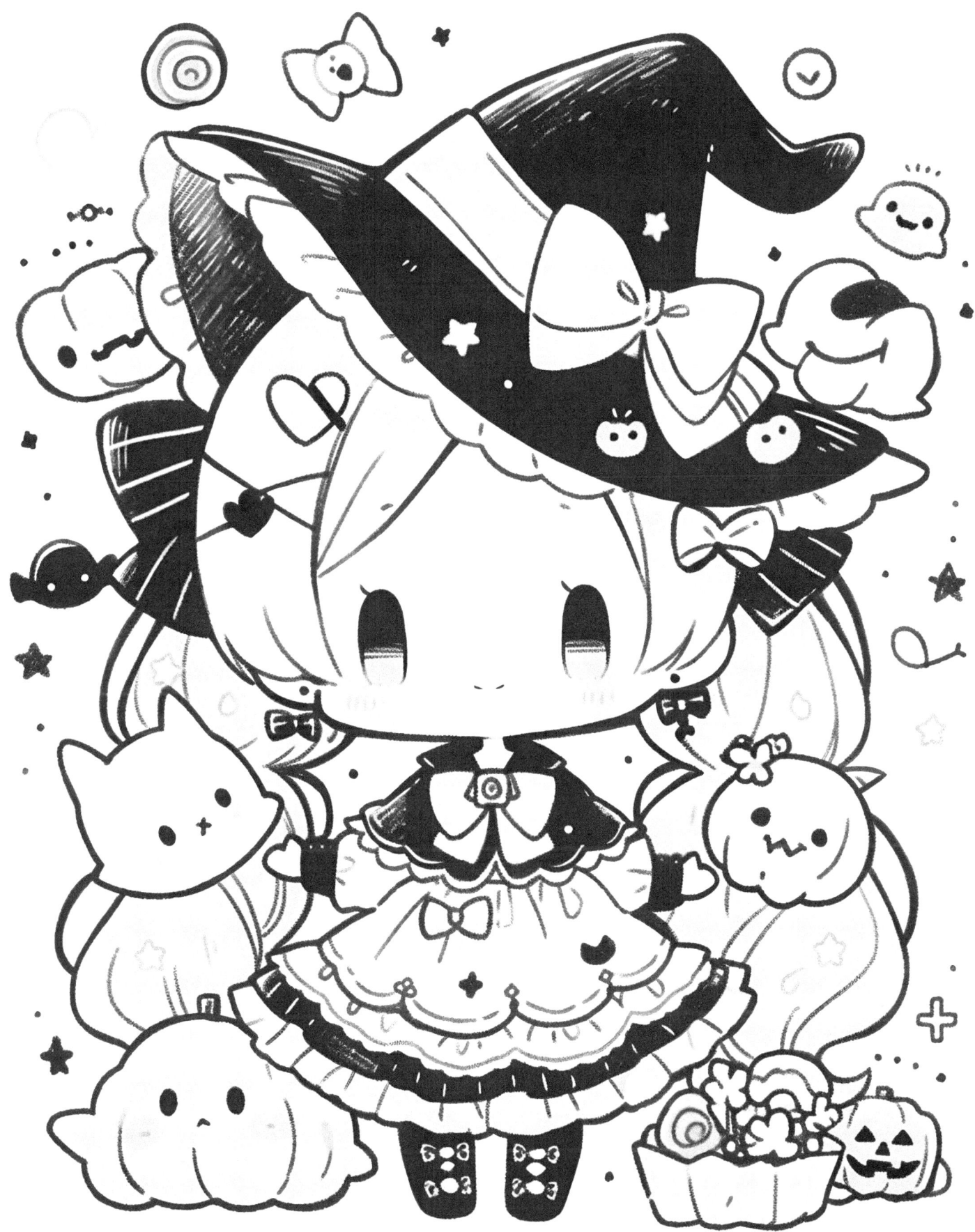

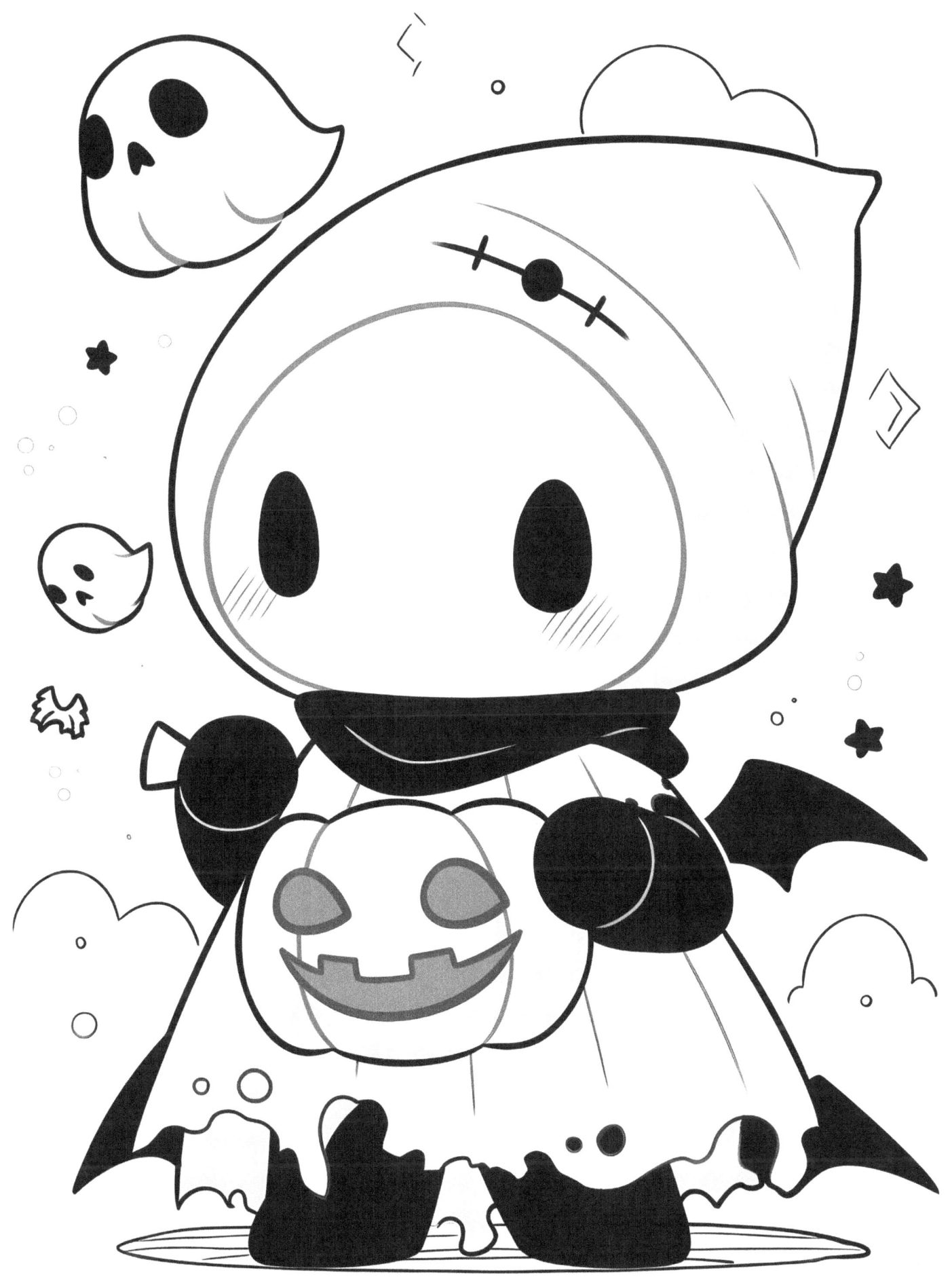

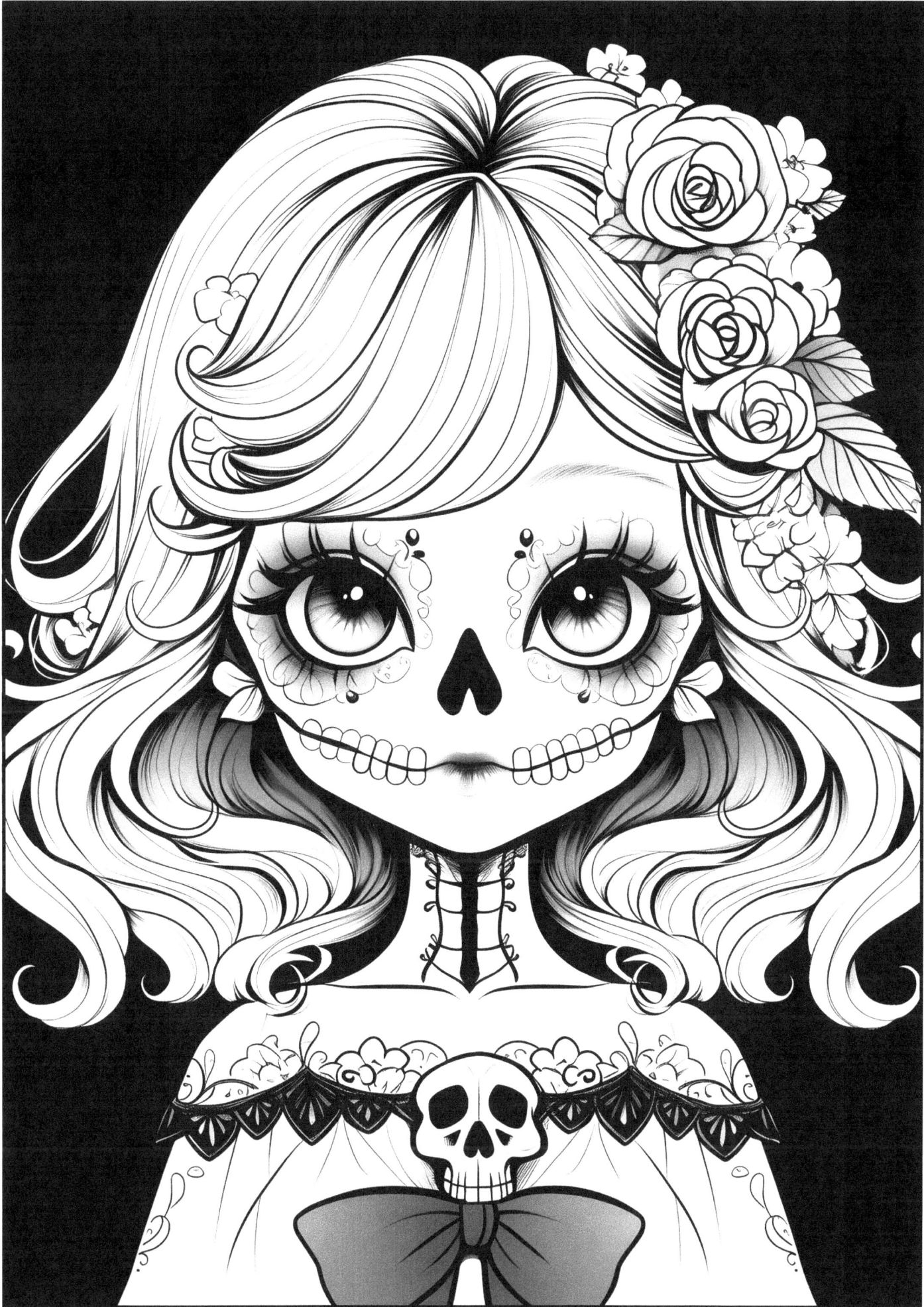

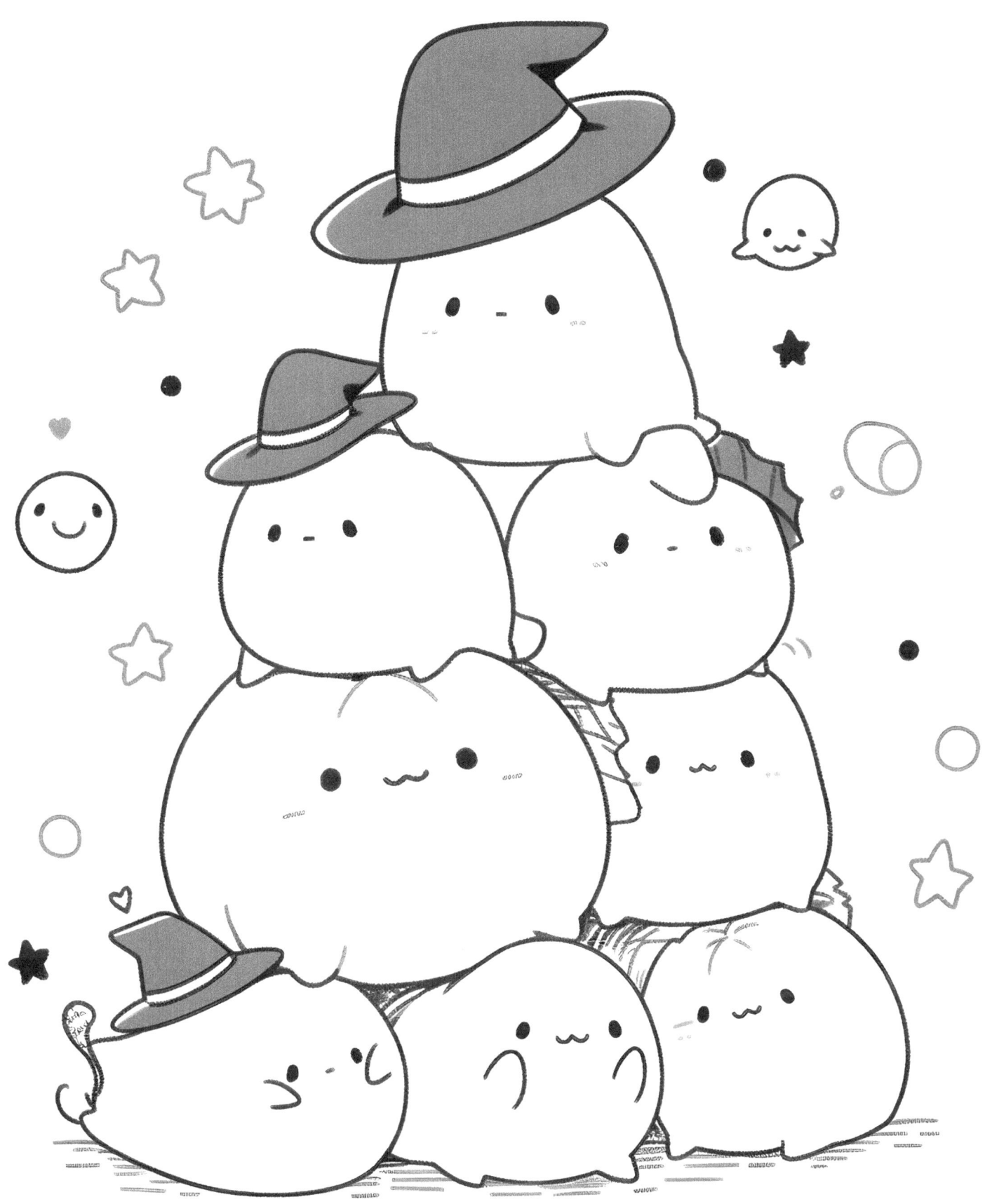

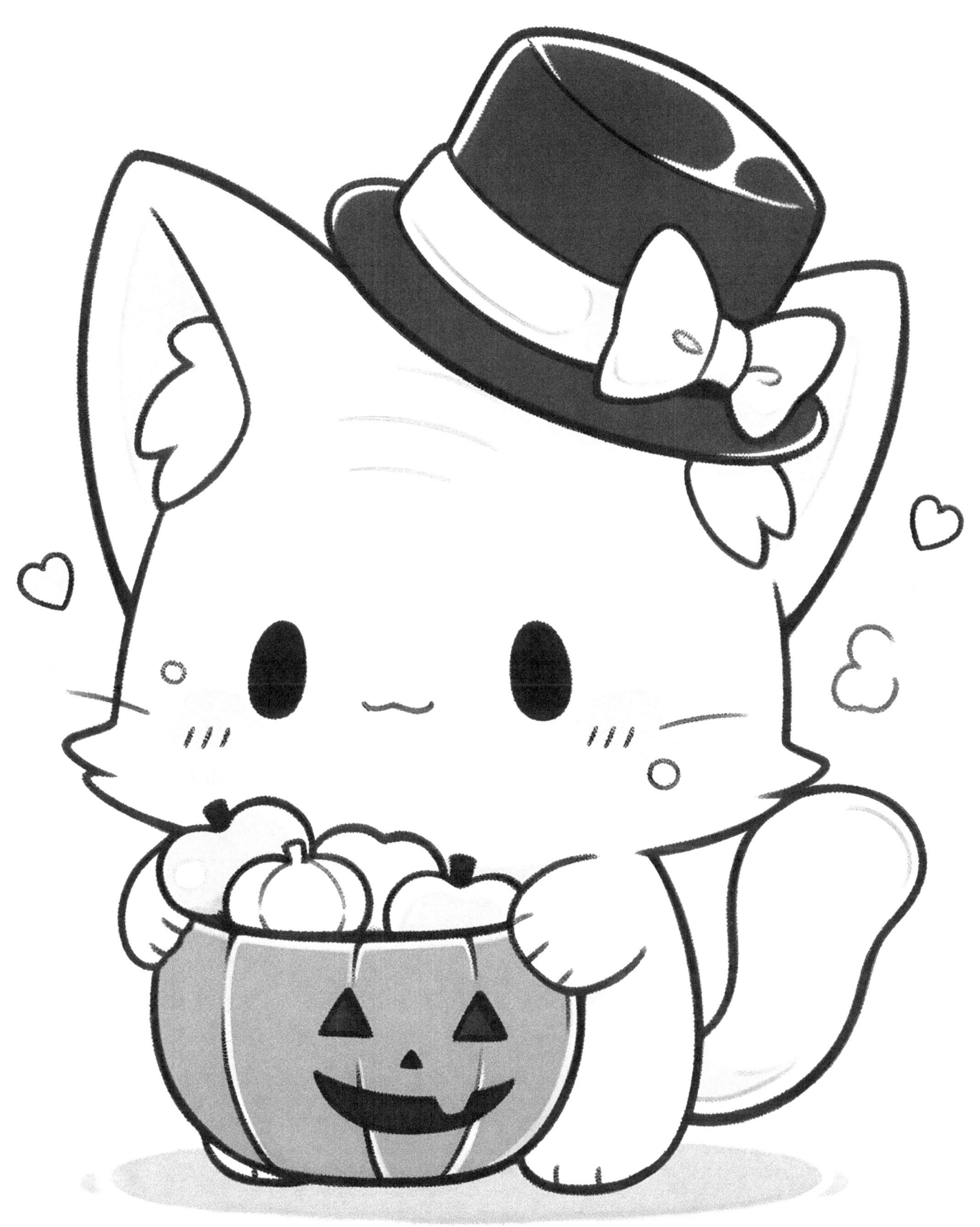

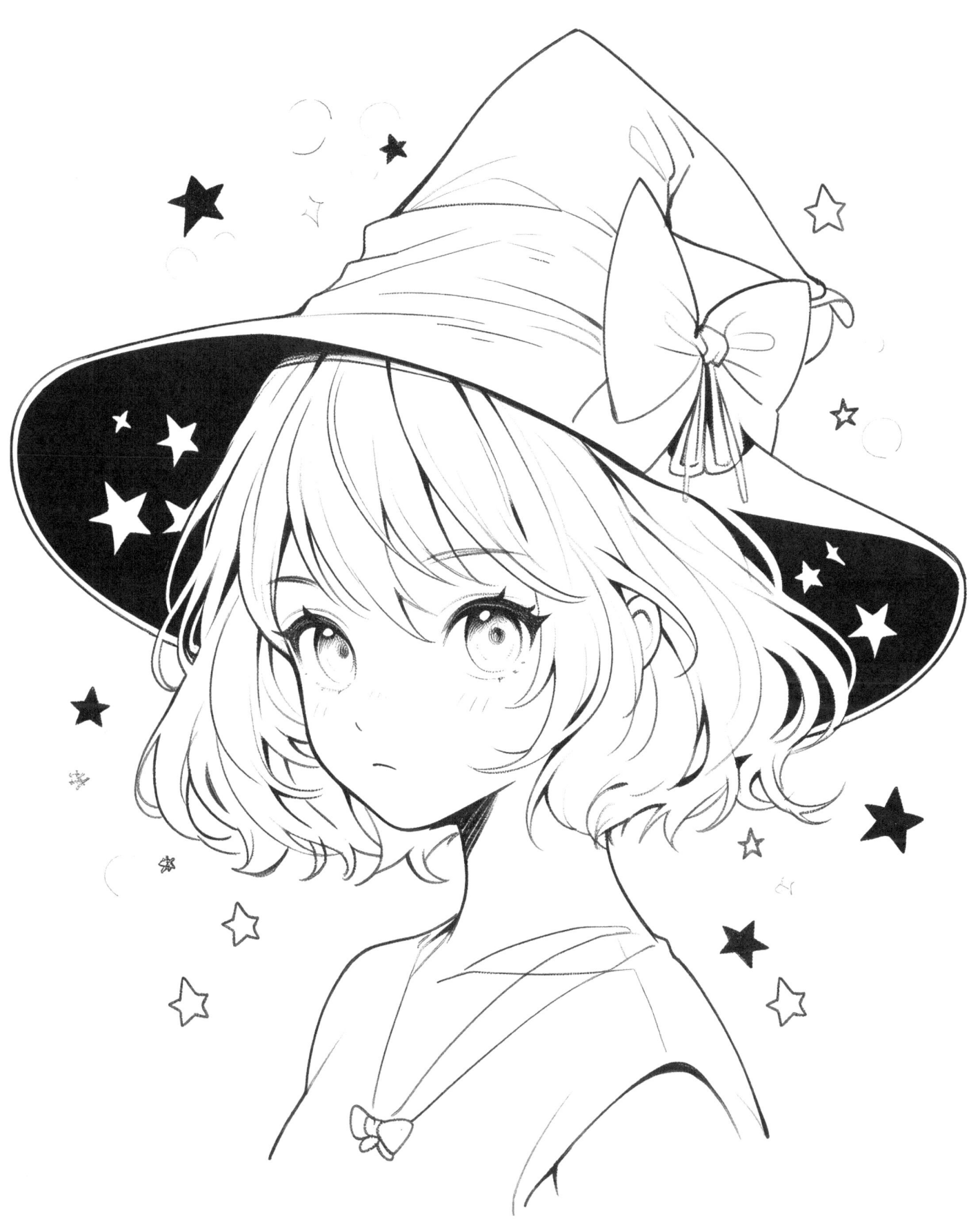

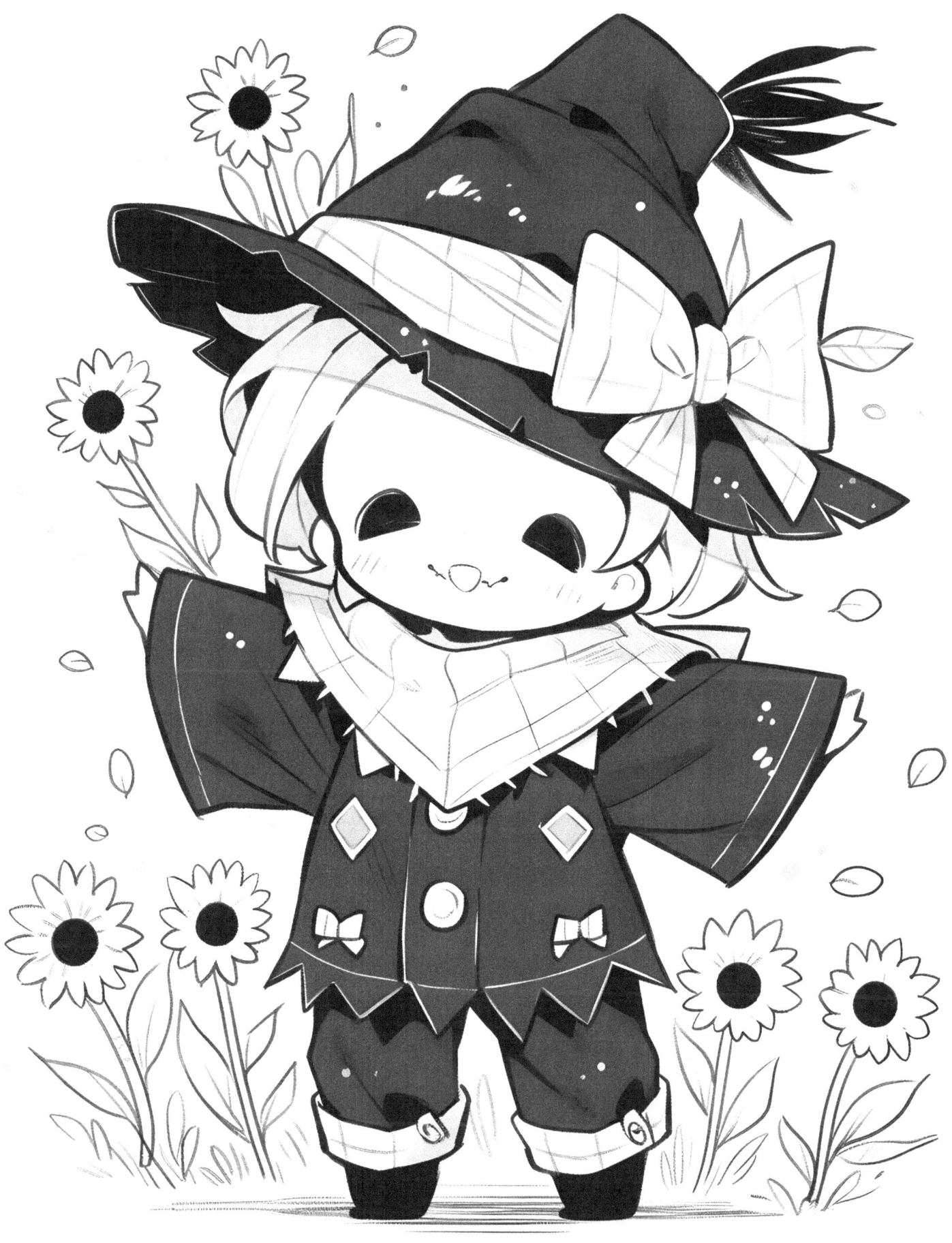

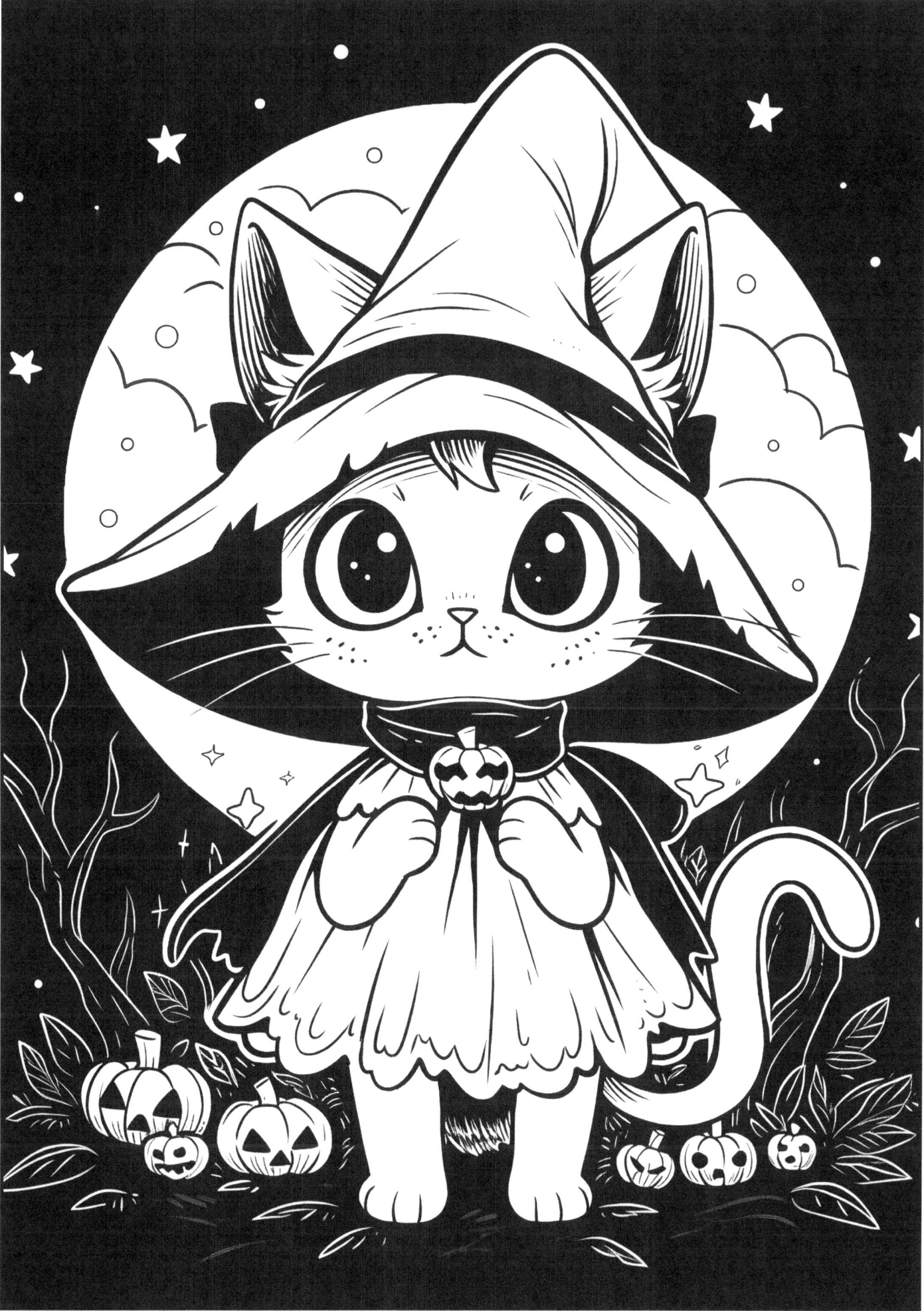

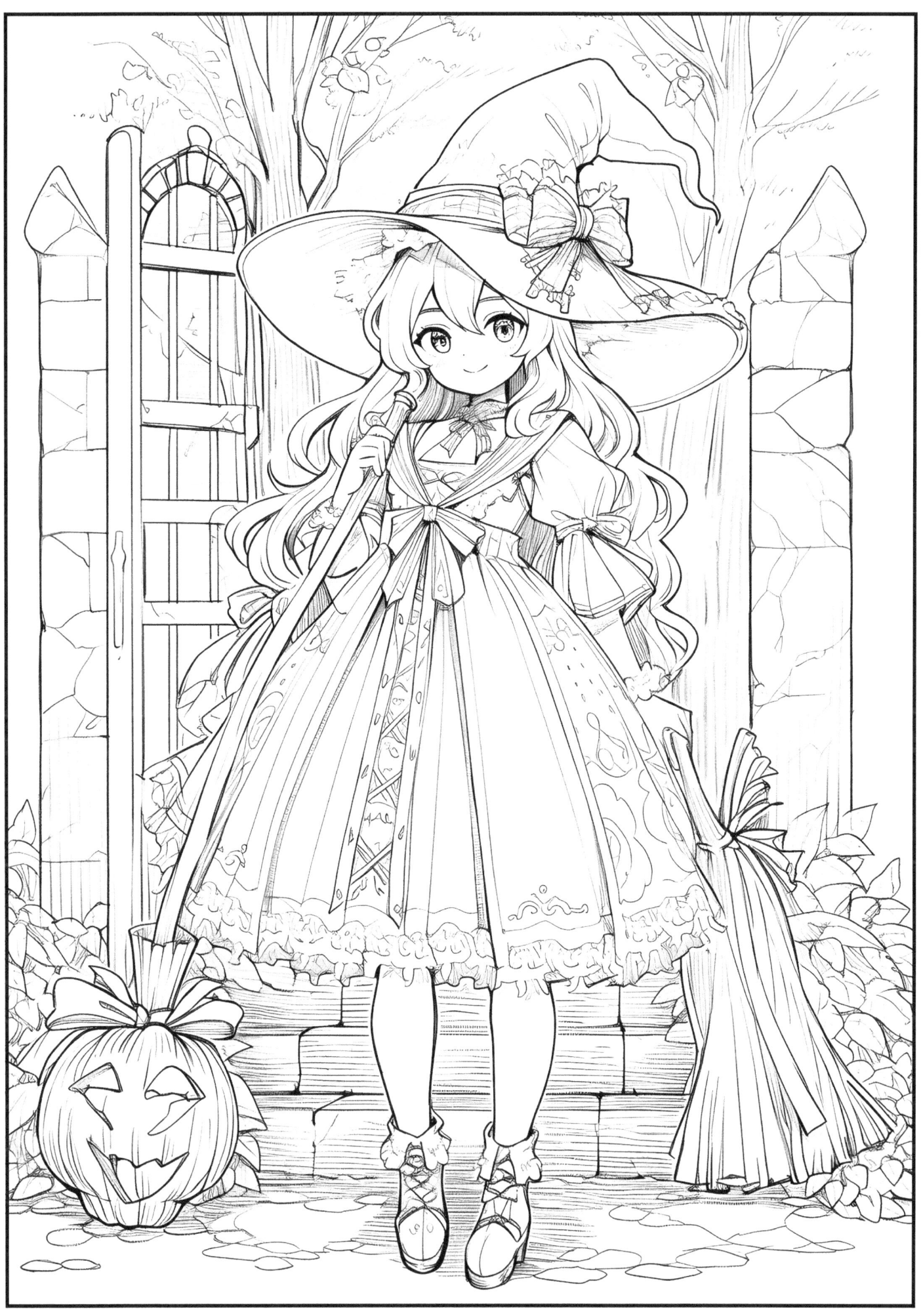

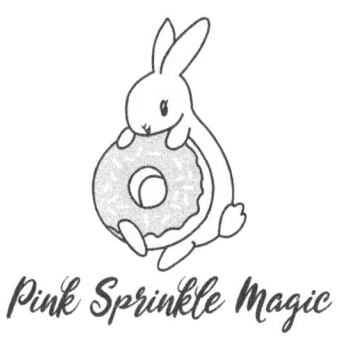

Pink Sprinkle Magic

Keep coloring and having fun!

Discover more cute kawaii coloring books:

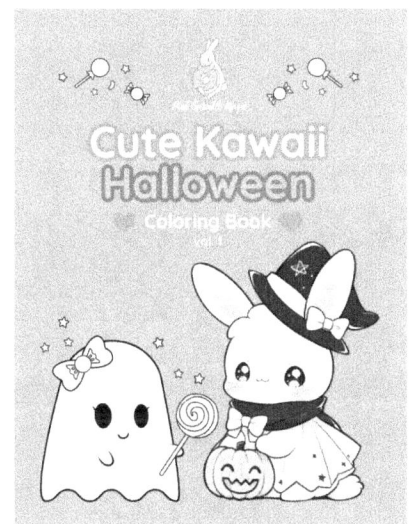

Halloween vol. 1

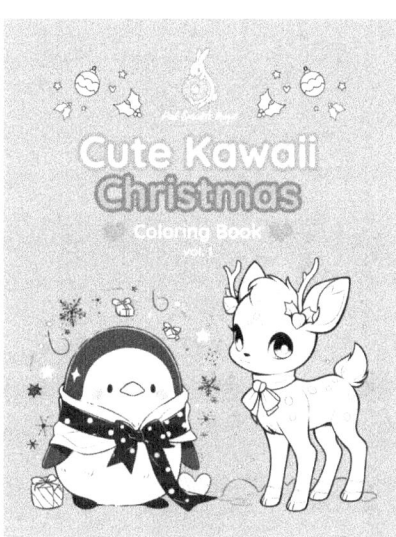

Christmas vol. 1

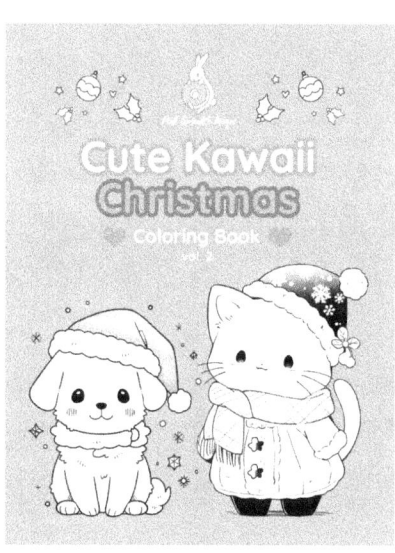

Christmas vol. 2

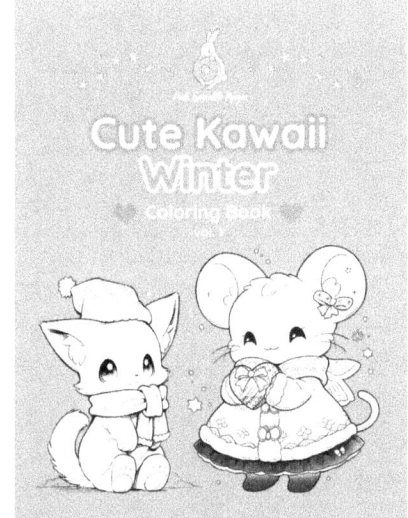

Winter vol. 1

Available on Amazon.com

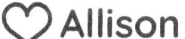

Thank you for supporting my dream of creating cute coloring books. I hope this book brings a sprinkle of magic to your day!

♡ Allison

Allison Haskins, creator of PinkSprinkleMagic

PinkSprinkleMagic.com